Electric Sunrise

Olivia Aguilar

Presentation by *BookLeaf Publishing*

Web: www.bookleafpub.com

E-mail: info@bookleafpub.com

ISBN: 9789358737141

First edition 2024

For that 10/11 push I needed

ACKNOWLEDGEMENT

It's quite possible to thank all of the inspirations who have walked in and out of my life for these poems. You are all an extension of my creativity. The only possible way to start to thank you is to keep writing to carry our stories out there.

PREFACE

Many of these poems have not seen the light of day. Actually. I have written more than half of these poems in the middle of the night when the house rested. I was the only source of life stirring in the hours between midnight and 3am. And sometimes the best way to see light is to sit in the dark in front of your laptop with a cup of coffee.

My Maker

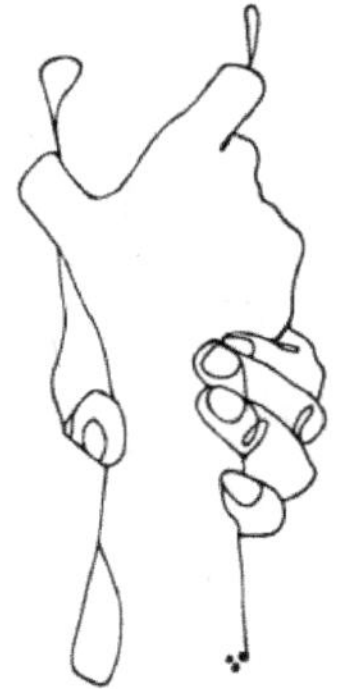

This ancient terror is equal to everyone
The only difference is how many times
It will welcome me as it almost did before
Like an old classmate
Who wants to know
What you've done with your life
In reality, it knows
And will continue to know
I'll put it off for as long as possible
Like I have the choice
Until I can no longer deny what awaits everyone
But I will be comforted by the thought
That I will not be the only one
I just hope it's not impatient to meet me
Because death must remember
Life is just as important

Don't Stop Me Now

I didn't think the first time would be just that
Not the last
I don't think about how I continued
or what would happen if I chose to stop
It's casual, they're sitting in my jar, staring at me
I know I won't stop doing it
It has helped me get through it
Having them stare at me every day,
Gives me ideas for my collection
It's just another good story to share with my
friends starting with,
"Well, there was this one time…"

Anti-fragility

When my vision, so narrow
Cannot see anything better,
I will stay in the tall grass
To obscure my vision
But the grass was only greener
Where others have stood
I don't dare to step out
I would only betray myself
A deserted path would follow my footsteps
Where I expected a bloom
An exposed patch of weeds are rooted
But I confess…
I don't know how I'll want anything else

Life's Melody

It's an echo
An attempt to seek communication
And in the midst of it
All those unanswered questions
Bounce back
Resounding silence
No response
Confirmation that you are hearing yourselves
correct
Remaining the same
Overtones of the good and bad
Let it happen
Let it take its course
Then repeat
Until you finally rest

My Entirety pt. 2

It makes me ache all over
Not because of the temperature
But because of the memories
And I'm afraid my memories have betrayed me
In more ways than one
Because certain people are no longer in them
I don't recognize the figures dancing in them
The aches irritate my comfort
Not because of the temperature
But because strangers are dancing like me
And I don't know if it's real

No Vacancies

I go home to empty pedestals
What once was, is not
But perhaps it never was
Perhaps it was someone else the whole time
Disguised, untruthful
And waiting to be discovered
The dust settles as time drags on
But no one is coming back
Despite expectations
And now
It's my turn to be on the pedestal

Strands

Melted there, eyes shut
Frozen in love
Too many things were happening
All at once, all at me
But keep talking to me
So I stay tethered here
So I don't drift away and get lost in the waves
But you'll let it happen
And I'll deal with the aftermath
When you're not around
When it's more convenient
That's what I do
When I find love
Where it wasn't supposed to be

Sideline

Back and forth
I don't lose sight on want I want
But my eyes tire of the movement
Even though my voice cheers your name
I will sit in the same spot
Even though I know you don't look for me
anymore
It's just in case I forget
You're looking in a different spot now
But I cheer just as loud
Deep in my heart I know
I'm still on your side

I'm a Goner

My heart pumped quicker than usual
No one was around
No option for suspense
It's quite scary
When someone has an effect on you
Without being there
When you think you can't give anymore
There goes your heart
Over and over again it goes
Pumping to the cadence of their voice
It doesn't know better
They laugh and you laughed harder
Louder
My heart was pumping quicker
They were around and watching
It's quite scary
When someone has that effect on you

When you have nothing left
They reach in and take more
It's theirs now
Because we are fleshy parts
Not knowing when to stop

To Haven

I'm passing time in his arms
As all my parts are hugged together
Until that cracking goes away
And there's no more places for my tears to
escape
The comfort is all I need
Because when I hug him
I don't have to look at everything he's done
But the rivers soon follow
So talk me back into your arms
And I'll be back
With a warning sign
That if you hug me enough
It will awaken some sense in me
That I'm not where I'm supposed to be

Wilted Attempt

Time that withers you also withers me
Trapped
Like sand in an hourglass
And I'll use you as a gauge
To see how I'm weathering the storm
I will not lose sight
But time does not flow the same way for all
I used you as gauge
But now I don't have a visual
The storm is harsher this time around
If you can do it
I'll somehow try to keep up
Because life has me in the palm of its hand
Threatening to lose me
Between its fingers
You've held on
So will I
Like sand in an hourglass

Time will lessen for the both of us
But time that withers you
Has withered me

Peripheral Absence

I can no longer stand in your truth
Even though it made sense at one point
I can no longer stand in front of you
But next to you
To try and understand why
To try and make sense
Of the pain, the guilt
Of being overwhelmed
Of being avoidant and quiet
The picture is much different being next to you
And we're looking at the same things
But you will still choose to walk away from me
That's the downside of being next to you
I won't see you walk away
But I will feel your presence slowly retreat
To find find someone else to stand in front of
you

Enough Sense

Please don't avoid me
Because it's not just about me
Love was found
Where it wasn't supposed to be
At least
That's how it felt
So what will be the cost of my honesty
Of this rush of relief
When I voice desires from my chest
My hands will betray me
Every time
Revealing I want something else
But I feel as though if I talk just enough
I will stop making any sense
Perhaps that's how it's supposed to be
Mint flavored sweet nothings
Because it's all about you
And not just about me

So please don't lose sight
Because I will lose my mind
And my body will follow someone else
Then my heart will have to pump hard
To get my eyes out of your lost and found
So avoid me
Because I wasn't where I was suppose to be

Slow Burn

Sometimes you don't know how deep you are
Until everything is about them
You stay there because you sense they're still
around
Waiting for you to come back
Or waiting a miracle
Because sometimes someone's tendency to
misplace things
Attracts someone with an unnatural ability to
find it

An Affliction

I have been plagued with this feeling
That people are a constant inspiration to me
There will always be an emotion to be printed
To be written a different way
From a different point of view
Every year my prescription changes
There's a new lens to look through
And this overwhelming feeling I succumb to
To look at someone and want to create
Because how could I not?
I would do myself a disservice to not document

To not remember how I felt in their presence
How overcome I was
To stop talking and start writing

I have been plagued with this feeling
That I'm not done writing
Because I will always encounter people
That will remind me of other people
And then another, reminding me
That I'm not done writing
This stream of endless encounters
That makes my hand find a pen, a napkin at least
And write until they are no longer in my view
And even then
I couldn't stop
I can't stop

Buzzed

I didn't know it was real until we touched
Electricity introduced itself into my bloodstream
The first couple months could've powered an
entire county
We spent it like we owned it and I felt it
Because my wanting generated new habits
Like second nature
But the bill was high

My Entirety

I will take you everywhere I go
Because I didn't have a choice
Because you left me with certain parts
That have now build parts of me

And now you're a part of my creation
I am made of countless people
And they have a part of me
So when we meet up again,
You will see
Which parts of you I kept

Midnight Strike

I'm getting ready
And this is what I have to do
To have all the pieces fall into place
But it might not be enough
Because that would be too soon
They're not ready to receive
So I'll overdo everything
Go overboard
But it might be too much
Because some people get overwhelmed
What else do I have to do
To make sure I do everything right
Because I'm afraid I'll lose the butterflies in my
stomach
So I'll fall asleep with roses in my hands

From The Backseat

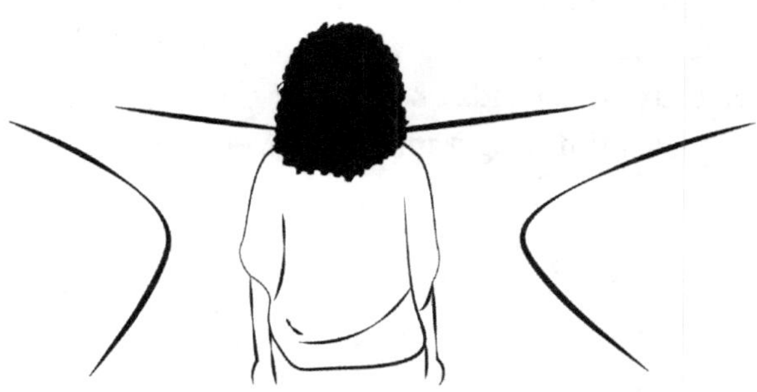

Watching everything come into view
It's happening right in front of you
It's happening away from you
And you watch
But it's not for you
You've been watching it happen at you
Happening all around you
Like everything is revolving around you
Yet it's not affected by your presence
And you watch
Watching everything come into view
Because it is not reliant on you
It'll keep on

Everything comes into view
It's happening right in front of you
It's happening for you
And you watch
Because you know it's for you

It's happening all around you
Everything is revolving around you
Magnetized by your presence
And you'll watch everything come into view
Because it depends on you
Now it's time to get into the driver's seat